All That is Left

Judith Harway's poetry has appeared in dozens of literary journals, as well as in *The Memory Box*, a chapbook published by Zarigueya Press in 2002. Her work has earned fellowships from the Wisconsin Arts Board, the Hambidge Center and the MacDowell Colony. She is on the faculty of the Milwaukee Institute of Art and Design.

All That is Left

Poems by Judith Harway

Turning Point

© 2009 by Judith Harway

Published by Turning Point
P.O. Box 541106
Cincinnati, OH 45254-1106

ISBN: 9781934999523
LCCN: 2009902289

Poetry Editor: Kevin Walzer
Business Editor: Lori Jareo

Visit us on the web at www.turningpointbooks.com

This is a work of fiction. Except for a few details borrowed from the author's family history, incidents, names, and characters are imaginary.

Acknowledgments

Some of these poems first appeared in the following publications:

Cortland Review, "Free"
Elsewhere, "What's in a Name"
The Blue Jew Yorker, "A Picture of My Father"
The Journal of the Wisconsin Academy of Sciences, Arts, and Letters, "The Only Jewish Family in the Neighborhood"
Whose Voice in the Mirror, an anthology published by Woodland Pattern Book Center, "Grandma's Kitchen"

"The Only Jewish Family in the Neighborhood" received an award from the *Wisconsin Academy of Sciences, Arts, and Letters, 2007.*

"My Grandmother's Babies" received a 2008 Muse Award from the *Wisconsin Fellowship of Poets.*

For both the material and moral support that has made this work possible, I am deeply grateful to the Hambidge Center for the gifts of time and silence; to the Wisconsin Arts Board for its 2007 Fellowship in Literature; to the Milwaukee Institute of Art and Design, especially my colleagues and friends (one and the same category) in Liberal Studies; to my critique group for inspiration, insight, and endless good company; and to my Renshi sisters, especially Kay Byer and Susan Lefler.

For my real-life parents
and grandparents,

For Dan,

For Sylvie and Keith
the future for us all.

Table of Contents

"And then,
we'll go wake our dead
with the life they bequeathed us
and we'll all sing together..."

— Gioconda Belli

The Golem

In Jewish folklore, a golem is an artificial person who is given life when a sacred word is carved upon its forehead.

From your ancestors' garden, dig a lump of clay:
how else to shape the past? Cup your hands

to mold a rough globe, squeeze a nose,
poke in an eye or two, then with a stick

gash any mouth you want. And it will do
because which of us, after all, does not find beauty

where we look for it? Always, our grandmothers
have read sacred names across our foreheads; always

our grandfathers, dust to dust, have known each breath
we draw is covenanted to our Maker. In every particle

of matter, says the Kabbalah, lies meaning:
crumbs and drops of what the world is

adding up to seas, to plants, to animals, to human
minds, to names and promises that someday

somebody like me would wake at birth
and never taste the bitterness of bondage. It will do

because it is the best we can do. Like my grandmothers
since time's first cry, I have borne my babies, cradled

shifting continents of bone above their brows, kissed
cheeks too full, a tiny pinch of nose, and prayed

that somehow this time life not make the features
hard. Yet which of us has not a soul

earned through suffering and mitzvot? If God can hear
each seed's suggestion that a wisp of green

is pleasing, and a leaf or two, how could He not hear
when a golem with a face like mine sings out

Baruch atah adonai? Still, I have only moved my lips
in silence by the Ark as my grandparents' great-grandchildren

are called to the Torah, singing like all history
depends on them, as it will do. The words unlearned,

unearned, uncarried by my voice, the melodies that wander
light as breeze through gardens where whatever loves

a shadow stirs — these I draw into my lungs,
kneeling among the roots, damp rising in my bones

like memory of what I might have known, of what
I might have prayed (had I been born at all),

had my grandparents not risked everything for me.
My hands dig loose, rich soil. I meet their living eyes.

I.

"And thou shalt speak unto him, and put words in his mouth; and I will be thy mouth....."

—Exodus 4:15

At the End of Life

When he could no longer raise
his head to look them in the eye,
Solomon shuffled away
from the well-wishers, aunts
and in-laws, their redundant pots
of soup and knishes, and retired
to his bedroom where he sat trembling,

his face a mask of absence.
Let his wife, whose tiny kitchen
brimmed with better food, accept
their sympathy: when they were gone
she'd taste the broth and season it
her way, with extra sage and onions.
This was his tonic: soup so savory

my pen stirs even now the rich
particulars of scent and taste,
of golden chicken fat and celery,
of how she ladled it into a chipped bowl
painted with pink roses, how she sliced
the challah, set the Shabbat candles
on his tray. In their small bedroom

where, years later, I would lie awake
my grandfather sat waiting.
Chaiele, he'd whisper,
and she'd shush him, blowing
on the soup as if he were a child.
She'd spoon it to his lips and dab them

with a corner of the napkin

laid across his white dress shirt
to catch broth and drool. Soon evening
murmured in. She would not light
the lamp. A wash of shadow
blurred the angles of her features,
smoothing worry lines and crows feet,
showing him again the village girl

who filled his heart: his Chaie
only ten years old the morning
she was caught beneath the table
eavesdropping as he tutored
her five brothers. She had practiced
Torah verses in the attic while
her sisters slept. She could sing

them still, that long gone afternoon
she caught his eye again
on Orchard Street, a world away,
a maiden now, her thin voice calling
from a place he thought he'd lost
forever. Beneath a flowered shawl
draped over head and shoulders,

her unruly curls and dark eyes made him
want to crush his owlish spectacles
beneath his heel. The rest,
the saying goes, is history:
she'd close her dark red album
at my bedtime on a past seasoned
her way, so savory and rich

I'd lie awake to taste even regrets,
to picture how he looked at her
even at the end of life, when all the soup
was gone, the pillows fluffed,
the Shabbat candles burning down to ash
and my grandfather slipped into dreams,

a napkin spread across his broken heart.

Shoes in Meskaporichi

In winter old men spend their days
gazing out at the street, the children cry
inside. No one has money. Shoes
are for the wage earners. The porters haul
their wood-wheeled carts like oxen,

rags binding what remains of soles
and uppers; even in their sleep, they cradle
their old boots. To keep his family, a man
must come to terms with cobblestones that gnaw
through leather soles in six weeks' time:

to hawk his wares, to haul his loads,
to walk with all the other men
to shul, to bring his son to cheder,
where he'll learn to follow in his fathers' steps.
Only the man with no legs needs no shoes:

from dawn to dusk, the crude cart bearing him
through what pogromschiks left him
of his life parks by the roadside
while his son bends to a tumpline, shoulders
loads of wood. Nearby, inside his dim shop

sits the shoemaker who stitches day and night.
Somehow he buys his leather. Somehow
customers with nothing buy his shoes:
what is a man to do but take each step
if he's to carry on?

Before the Pogrom

Early spring.
A dark room lit
by candles. Children
on the floor before
a smoky hearth,
toes of their shoes
cut off for growing.
Smells of soup
and cabbage,
damp socks hung
to dry. Straw mattresses
piled high with winter
quilts. Outside, a shawl
of rain drawn over
evening's face. Flocks
of goats lie huddled
on the leaky sod
of rooftops, handcarts
turning home
down muddy lanes.
A gathering of relatives
who stare into
the slow shutter of history,
afraid to move.

At Pesach
the Haggadah tells us
of a time of bondage,
of the flight
of the Israelites from Egypt

into the wilderness
of freedom. Plagues
rained on the land.
The hand of the Almighty
smote even babies
dead. This is the way
I understand the day
my grandmother's family
left Meskaporichi:
there never was a choice:
A journey starts
when it is time to go.

Affidavit of the Master or Commanding Officer

I, Chief Officer of the **Kursk**, from **Libau**
do solemnly, sincerely, and truly **Swear**
that I have caused the surgeon of said vessel

to make a physical and oral examination
of each and all of the steerage Aliens named
in the foregoing Manifest Sheets, **40** in number,

and from the report of said surgeon
and from my own investigation, I believe
that no one of said Aliens is an idiot, or imbecile,

or a feeble-minded person, or insane person,
or a pauper, or is afflicted with tuberculosis
or with a loathsome and dangerous disease,

or is a person who has been convicted of, or who admits
having committed a felony or other crime
involving Moral turpitude, or is a polygamist,

or an anarchist, or a prostitute, or a woman or girl
coming to the United States for the purpose
of prostitution, or for any other immoral purpose,

and that, according to the best of my knowledge
and belief, all the information in said Manifests
concerning each of said Aliens named therein

is **Correct and True** in every Respect.

Free ...

—Solomon, sailing into New York Harbor

as, to court the obvious, a bird
one of the raucous swirl
diving for offal in the steamship's wake

as young men doff their hats and crush
against the rail, stunned by the engines'
lurch towards silence, a dull humming

after nineteen days of roar; or free
as sunlight, pale and hesitant, an aura
petaling the Statue on her island,

bigger than imagining. A free ride
yours, across the North Atlantic
hiding first in folds of darkness

down below then slowly learning
that a man can be so quiet
no one notices the absence of his name

upon the manifest. Free as the bread
of strangers, weevily potatoes; free
as tears, as prayers that praise God freely

though you ask him nothing.
"Land of the Free," a crust of island
rises to meet the ship like certainty

you've nothing left to lose, you're free
to take your chances, for good or ill, in this
the only world I've ever known.

Tending the Past

—for Chaie

Wrap your feet in rags. Come stravaging
home down a lane between potato fields
as daylight waters down to dusk
and hearthstones stir with fire. Take off

your shawl. Bend to your stitchery
by candlelight, pretending not to laugh
at your brothers singing *Etel Betel's tochter*
und Chaim Yankel's zohn. Unpin your hair

and brush it to your waist at bedtime.
It is better not remembering
some names, some times: just drop them
like a glove, their loss unnoted

in the mystery of how this world rolls
over us. Rolled in the same old quilt
wake up a million miles away
from Meskaporichi. Though home

is all you see, even with closed eyes,
bend to your stitchery until the whistle sounds
then shuffle out into grey streets
where lamps already glow. Walk slowly

in your flowered shawl and listen
past the cartwheels' clatter, shouts and horns,
the streetcars' racket down the Bowery
for a voice as gentle as your father's was

then take a man from home and love him well.

Take his name, although its syllables pile up
like fallen chimney stones. Brush out your hair
and sow the rugs of your apartment

with hairpins and tears. Wrap your son in songs
you carried from the shtetl, feeding him
on things kept to yourself
no one can make you tell.

My Dearest Parents,

May these words find you
in health, blessed by my brother Avram's
safe return from Minsk. It grieves my heart
to bear this distance as you gather

sitting shiva for Grandfather, may he rest
in peace, whose wisdom filled the shul like song.
My father, you have written of the congregation
turning to him for brave words, for words

to sweep away the cold tracks of these times
outside your door. The story of our lives —
how many ways can one man tell it
to a minyan starved for miracles?

Ask me only once, and I will send you passage.
After these eight years I still dream every night
we're sitting down together, sharing tea and bread.
It grieves my heart to think I'll never gaze

again into the mirror of your eyes
and ask your blessing: Papa, Mama, soon I will
be married! She's a fine young woman,
daughter of the merchant Yossel (Do you remember him?

He sailed three years before me. Avram and I
tutored his five sons). She is my Chaie.
She is twenty-one. Her character is sewn, in every detail,
perfectly as tiny stars across the shawl of Heaven.

Bless your son, and hold me in your hearts
as I will hold my Grandfather, may he rest in peace,
and sing the sh'ma, my eyes closed tight
for every one of us.

Legacy

She left me what she could:
three hand-embroidered blouses,
her red rocking-chair, an ancient quilt
stitched over woolen batting,
random photographs, and strange to say,
a pair of satin bloomers. She left me
half her money, too, six hundred dollars,
I should save it for the child I carried.

Grandma passed when I was a young bride
but all her scraps of story cling
to me like lint; they cloud my sleep
with charms and spells for not forgetting.
I must have been sixteen the day
she drew a small box from her dresser drawer,
unburying a picture at its heart. It shook me
like water from the leaves:

a girl who could have been my age,
could have been me, in fact
sat on a table, long hair hanging wild
from one side of her bandaged head, naked
above the waistline of her gathered skirts.
She leaned into the arms
of an old woman but she faced the lens
her gaze expressionless, or maybe

challenging someone like me
to pray for her. *This was after the pogrom*
my grandmother said, her fingertips

caressing every gash and hollow,
awful tears of flesh, as if to heal them.
She's your grandfather's sister.
I couldn't help but wonder
at her ordinariness: the day before

perhaps she'd grumbled at her chores,
told her mother a half-truth
(like I did) when she came home late.
So as not to see her wounds
I met the picture's eyes
as if through a night window
where my own reflection still floats
on the pane, and hers within it.

Last Words

If not for memory, what is
my life? I still remember
how my mother's arms
plunged down the well's dark throat,
to draw the bucket back, hand
over hand, to daylight. Water sloshed
her skirts. I'd lean too far to see
what I could not: the mossy walls,
the living water's surface
where I longed to float
beneath a round of sky,
to gaze up all day long at stars
it held for me. Below the earth
I dreamed of drifting, below
the wagon wheels and shouts,
the oxen lowing, below hoarfrost
and mud and shivering
with cold, the dull ache
in my gut, below being
afraid. This is eternity,
I'd think, this dream of quiet
so complete my life began again
and ended in its depth.

What I was Told

The day Sol died was no different from any other
day. His wife washed and shaved him, helped him

to his chair so she could change the sheets. Sun funneled down
the air shaft, casting shadows from the fire escape

like black and white keys on the wall. Outside, kids called,
trucks backfired, something banged, and nothing mattered

to him but the fact of one small room he hadn't left
in weeks. He'd sold the candy store. The world had gone to hell,

his son came home from the War, what more could life deliver?
He still could stand; he still could shuffle to the mirror.

What he longed for were the things he couldn't do:
walk streets entombed in memory, write postcards home

to ghosts, sleep soundly as his life burned down
to ash and tallow. One man can hold off night

only so long. Since I know better than to tell
the truth, I'll tell what I was told: his wife came home

to find him dead. The family gathered. In a florid hand,
the death certificate reads, *Cause: Unknown.*

Books

Dostoevsky, Einstein, Buber, Marx
and Emerson kept company
with my grandfather in his last days
on Earth. In the red rocking chair
before the window he would sit,
a book laid open on the pillow in his lap,
his quaking hands hung at his sides
lest they should interrupt before
a new page needed turning.
Learning was the river he dived into
as a young man back at the Yeshiva
where the rabbis always spoke
in questions. Now it was his turn to ask,
though what he hungered for
no longer was the Talmud: *If man*
created God, how did the universe begin?
What is the nature of the soul? Can humankind
create a just society? Of course,
no one save he, Buber, and Einstein knew
of Sobibor, the trenches in the forest,
knew the world his dreams had haunted
since he left it forty years before
was lost. And Marx, whose words
once seemed to curve into a gleaming
future, maddened him these days.
And though sometimes he even felt
like telling Emerson to *shut up;*
life is hard, at last his days were rich
with time, the fertile ground
which his companions cultivated
with their pens. His whole adult life

my grandfather spent late nights
laboring over the books
for his brother's appetizing store,
the nut stand, his own candy store
and soda fountain, penning long columns
of numbers which, for the most part,
tallied loss: Einstein himself
came in once for an egg cream
in a year so lean they couldn't let him
have it on the house. So in the presence
of these great men, let me sit
a while. Let me turn pages,
light the lamp at dusk, and read
the better story of his death,
the one my father tells
in which his wife comes home to find
he's left her, glasses on his nose,
the book still open
to a passage that he loved.

Last Words

The moon's pale light
floods down between
apartment houses, bleak
and cold. It breaks
against my window.
My heart freezes shut.
The world we dreamed of
never was this world, in which
I mean to hurt you
who have loved me.
What is left of me? A bag
of bones, a voice
I dimly hear that calls
the dead to come home
and I follow. Even the stars
this cloud swept night
are buried in the sky.

Sol Bringing Flowers to Chaie

— *Caption for a photograph*

They sat talking on the porch so late last night
the universe cooled down to starlight and the mountains,
black against black, drew in close around them. Now
she's sleeping, drifting between life and somewhere
sweeter, as he dresses, walks up to the meadow,

walks away from himself as he exists every other week
of the year but this one at the bungalow, when the candy store
is closed and he enters into the perfect light of morning.
Breathing in, he feels the tipping of his heart
towards fullness. If he knew the names of columbine

and phlox, of bluebells and wild iris, he'd compose
a love poem, but he only knows she loves
a mix of colors. I can almost hear what he hears,
birdsong punctuated by the neat tap
of his walking stick, and maybe he will hum

a tune he'd forgotten until something in the whispering
of meadow grasses wakes the past. He appears so small
in his white knickerbockers, his full moon glasses
giving him a look of eternal surprise, clutching the nosegay
in his right hand with the walking stick. If only

the morning of this photograph could happen over
and over again, until they are old, the way his life was told
to me in childhood, the way it should have been;
if only, after three decades of marriage, she would not wake up

to the blood of his wrists blooming red and wild.

Last Words

For days I've sat here wondering
how else to leave you
and no passage opens:
if only life could switch off
like a light, or, with a tug
of thread simply unravel.
If only death sold tickets
like a streetcar. What choice
have I? You lock away
my medicines, you watch me.
How can I forgive myself
for what you'll see,
for how you'll beg the coroner
to lie? Our souls
are not our own to take,
the rabbi says, but I know
there are worse things
a man can do
than steal away.

What's in a Name

My Grandma says that no one, *no one*
in the whole wide world has our last name
but us. My father checked the phonebook
all five boroughs: not a single stranger
with our name. His father lugged our name

through Ellis Island in his bag. Penniless,
it smells of schmaltz and boiling cabbage.
I can hear it clang each time my father
slams the black cage door, the elevator groans
and I feel sure we're trapped forever

or we'll fall. My friends have common names
and grandmothers who speak correctly,
wear white gloves and lipstick, never curse
in Yiddish. Mine makes the elevator stink
without leaving her kitchen.

But her kitchen, says my father, keeps
her living. When she lifts the lid
to stir the soup, bouquets of steam escape,
her face glows damp and rosy like a baby's
as she laughs. She pours a drop of sweet wine

in a shot glass, my portion, a child should taste the past
she says like it's important. It's OK with me
my Grandma tells the same old stories every visit,
never mind the details shift like clouds:
her village, Meskaporichi, is a little world

that drops down from the heavens
into mine. It's not a pretty place.
The streets are rank and muddy. Everyone
is poor, their raggy clothes like sack-cloth,
but the rabbi wears a long black flappy coat,

his fur hat bobbing as he skirts the puddles.
Grandma's Solomon, my dead grandfather
studied to be a rabbi. Such a brilliant boy,
she says, and kind, though his heart was too light
for tending the Eternal. And in the Pale

the Holy Books were all a Jew could read.
Neither could he own his land or travel,
and Jewish men the army took away
seldom came home. Grandma's eyes pool up
with candlelight and sorrow. She was near my age

she says, when soldiers came for Solomon's brother.
Now she hides her face behind her hand
like praying, and I picture Sol
walking out alone into the marsh. The night is deep
and still. His body folds into itself with fear

and every star that looks down on him flutters
like his heart. Not even the rabbi knows
he dreams of leaving.
                                        In his pocket, Sol conceals
a grimy clutch of documents that keeps him

from conscription. The way she tells this part,
I think my Grandma loved him all her life:
she says he saw the future glow like tiny wings
in amber, warming to his hands; she says a man's name

is as precious as his word. Her story ends

the same place mine begins: that night my grandfather
handed his name, his future, to his brother,
fled and stowed away across the North Atlantic
hiding in the shadows of a name no one remembers
now. Grandma clears the dishes and my father yawns,

it's time to leave. I close my eyes to wish
upon my dead grandfather's names like stars:
the one he lost, the one he found, the one
that's ours and no one else's in the whole wide world
he crossed to bring me safely home.

II.

"And in those darknesses I lay down
as conscious of my love for my
children as I would have been of
a sudden and chartless fever."

—Eavan Boland

Like Any Story

Here's a story, and like any story, it may be true
or not: fleeing their village, a mother hid her children
beneath a wagon load of hay. By night
they bounced on top, their hands and faces blushed
with cold; by day, a pale sun heckling the hay wagon,

they slept. The horses plodded on. The earth spun
four times round before they reached the border post:
a roadside shack, a handful of disheveled soldiers
and outside a hill of garbage for the dogs. Like any soldiers,

these were someone's sons but in that hinterland
they pinned the mother's arms, spat in her face;
they rocked the wagon, jabbing bayonets
into the nest of hay. Born at a sharp and bloody point
of history the children lay like death: I'm haunted

by their stillness as a steel blade grazed
the baby's cheek, another sliced the middle daughter's
skirts. The morning held its breath. The soldiers spat
and yawned; time wandered on its way again,

no one the wiser. Like any story, this one ends
wherever silence opens, where gaunt horses stir
against their tracings and a wagon labors on.
Like memory, a story's frontier shifts as slowly
as the course of stars with every telling, altering

constellations imperceptibly. Fleeing the shtetl,
my grandmother's mother hid her children, one way
or another, saving them and blessing me
with breath enough to tell it.

My Grandmother Talking

Have a piece of bread to that, already,
she'd say, handing me a plate of chicken liver
fried in schmaltz. *Eat. I can hardly see you.*
Decades after immigrating, English
remained slippery to her as herring

wavering in shallows. *V* and *W*
flipped on her tongue: *You vant, perhaps,*
some wegetables? all four syllables enunciated,
we-ge-ta-bles, because food is ritual
and never to be hurried. In her kitchen

daily life's subject and predicate were clear
as broth in which she boiled the chicken
to within an inch of its life, then lifted
the lid with a sigh as if facing
the sacred. My grandmother

believed that anyone she fed, if she spoke
slowly, understood her best in Yiddish.
So we chewed like a rhythm section
behind her memories of keeping goats
that grazed on the sod roof, of bolts of silk

that glowed like far-off moons
in a chest in her father's shop. I couldn't catch
the half of it, and half the time
I didn't try. Her stories looped
into a nebula of lace, but once I broke

the thread by asking was it 1912
the year she'd come from Russia.
1912? she cried, in English now,
It wasn't 1912. I'll tell you precisely:
It was a long, long time ago.

Thinking of Her While Touring Ellis Island

Who remained to say goodbye
        the day you left? What was the dearest thing
                you carried? If she couldn't read,

how did your mother find which ship
        of dozens on the wharves of Libau
                held her hopes? Did you have to claw

like animals for space? How did you use
        the toilet? Could you keep Shabbat
                in steerage? On stormy days

when no one went on deck, did you dream
        of the sky? Did your mother cry
                while you were still awake? When the ship docked

did you feel the warmth of Heaven underneath your feet?
        What if you'd been sent back?
                Who recognized your father

in the crowds and, after Meskaporichi,
        was the tenement he took you home to
                home? How many days were you a family

again before his death? If I embroider
        hearsay and invention on your life's
                plain linen, will your eyes look back

from any of my patterns? In this new world
you gambled on for my poor sake
show me how you began.

Grandma's Kitchen

Grandma's kitchen greeted you outside
the apartment door, gossiping of bread
still oven-warm, of brisket, cabbage
boiling (always cabbage boiling) and fried
onions, smells that wrapped the world she'd left
behind around her like a shawl. No one
could visit with her in its sacred space,
brimful already with her birdlike arms
and banging pots. She kissed us, scolding
Meine sheyne maidlakh, so thin
already — though she herself was thin
as a spoon, and stubborn —
You must be starving from hunger. Come,
sit down. I'd write a better life
for her, but always I come back to dinner
at the lacquered table, red and black,
the one memento of her wedding pressed
up to the couch. And dishes — lukshen kugel,
kreplach soup, the world she'd left behind
served steaming hot so she was not alone
with her blond grandchildren, the shiksa wife
her only son had wed. Grandma's kisses
smelled of lard and lotion as her fingers
gripped our faces, scared to let us slip
beneath night's billows in the bed
she'd shared with two dead husbands.
But it was late, the kitchen stacked
with pans. We fell asleep to the last music

of her dishwashing, and she sat up
to drink her tea before the kitchen's air shaft
window, where the ink of night
spelled every world she'd lost.

The Angel Who Keeps Away the Darkness

"Rabbi Mendel once boasted to his teacher Rabbi Elimelekh
that evenings he saw the angel who rolls away the light before the
darkness, and mornings the angel who rolls away the darkness
before the light. 'Yes,' said Rabbi Elimelekh, 'in my youth I saw that,
too. Later on you don't see these things anymore.'"
— Martin Buber

Mendel's was the candy store
at 161st Street and Gerard
we walked to, hand in hand,
my older sister and my grandmother
and me. The narrow shop was dim
as dusk. The smells of roasting nuts,

of chocolates cooling on the racks,
of citrus swirled around like dust
tornadoing through rays of sunlight
as the glass door opened, jingling
us in. Old Mr. Mendel, bent and bearded,
loomed behind the counter

like a phantom. Grandma told us
to choose anything we wanted, anything
at all: a bag of sweets, a pinwheel,
a pound of chocolate in a box
shaped like a heart, bouquets
of hair-ribbons, one of the crowd of dolls

hanged from the rafters overhead, or else
the lot of it. From down below,
the dolls' tableau unsettled me:
Who'd do a thing like this? Their eyes

were too wide open, glazed and sightless;
they wore pinafores and patent leather shoes

like mine, and I was getting blisters
pacing up and down beneath their feet,
bearing the weight of choice.
My sister, twirling on a soda fountain stool
already held a box of candy and a teddy bear,
and Mr. Mendel ladled streams of fudge

like magma on her ice cream sundae.
Anything at all. My room at home
had four dolls on the bed, and three more
in the closet; on my dresser, color wheels
of ribbons lay, and every night
before he tucked us in, my father

brought a dish of chocolate ice cream up,
or maybe cookies, we should have
a treat while listening to the nonsense
we loved best: *Two shoes, new shoes,*
bright shiny blue shoes... There was an old woman
who lived in a shoe.... I stood there

kicking at the dusty floor, as Mr. Mendel
beamed, my sister ate, the hot fudge
ear to ear. And Grandma waited for me
in her old cloth coat, her orthopedic shoes,
her flowered babushka, until I chose.
In Grandma's eyes, I never chose enough.

On the Subway

My white gloves bunched
        as I gripped Grandma's hand
like my last hold on Earth.
        She leaned down, ruffling

my pin-curls with her lips,
        her voice fragmenting
in the scream of steel wheels
        to another stop, then knocking

heads together we rocked on.
        I closed my eyes,
pretending nothing smelled
        of sweat and pee. Beyond my lids

a world of strangers swayed
        in strangers' arms; lights stuttered
fitfully like eyes of ghosts
        burning with old blind wishes

sad to lose their beauty
        and their lives. In Grandma's world
I thought, most everyone
        who mattered was already dead

except for me
        and I was very small.

From Her Red Album

Good years these were, she croons,
her dark red album open in her lap. *Come,*
sheyne maidlakh, sit with your Grandma.
Come see your Grandma
when she was a beauty.

Like gravity, her invitation
draws me. Her fingers, gnarled
as roots and slow as sleep,
leaf through discolored plastic sheets
that hold a sweeter world. She cannot

hurry: every snapshot matters,
every story blooms from eyes
long since gone dim. Can these be
my grandparents, these lovers
ripening in summer sun so clear

it almost breaks your heart?
Their ardor sweeps into the lens
like an onrushing storm:
here she reclines, a Lorelei
on rocks beside a stream, her earnest suitor

cradling her head as if there is no more
this life could offer; here they sit
together smiling on a garden swing,
and here they curl into each other's arms
beneath an arbor, gaze to gaze,

so certain of the treasure buried

in their hearts they know
no hesitation. *Such a couple,*
your Grandpa and me, she sighs
stroking his face as though the image

could be flesh again. *Back in the village*
even, I had eyes for him. She is smiling now.
She smoothes her hair, her cheeks flushed pink
with summer sun so strong it warms
the many seasons after.

My Grandmother's Babies

After she miscarried for the fourth time
an old doctor told her *You're too small.*
No child can grow inside you.

She took to her bed. She burned
and froze with grief. Her husband
called across the dark perimeter

she paced within her heart
but she ignored him, hearing only
melodies caught in a flute

no one will ever play.
Sometimes she'd rise
to stand before the mirror.

What it gave her back
was smaller still than she remembered
feeling: all those awful bones

jutting beneath her flesh, the hollows
of her eyes, a body longing to be buried
underneath the quilts

her mother gave her
when she was a bride. Day
after summer day, she listened

for the children wasting time
outside on stoops;
the double-dutch of afternoon

swirled into evening
as their mothers called them in
and she was left alone

cradling her little deaths.
As autumn came, the dry
unripened fruits hung in her heart

began to fall at last. Her husband
gathered in their shadows,
held her in his arms and gave her

what they did not even dare
to wish for anymore, a murmuring
like wings inside her womb. Her body

swelled and softened. Wrapping her
in quilts, he rubbed her feet,
her back. She heard him humming

lullabies as he brought in
her tray. Though fifty hours of labor
nearly did her in, a child —

my father — filled his lungs
with breath, his first cries drowning
in the silence of the lost.

Summer 1930, in the Catskills

— Sol and Chaie's boy

From the station, jitneys fetched
your family to the bungalows,
a scatter of tin roofs at the end
of a dirt track. Trunks and valises,
sacks of bread and cabbage, coats
despite the summer heat unloaded

in a pile your parents might have hauled
through Ellis Island. It was to be
a week in the country: a week
of mountain air, good for the lungs,
of picking blueberries and daisies.
A week of nights when only bullfrogs

cried their love aloud, no neighbors
on the air shaft. Your mother tied
your shoes with double knots.
Your father clutched your hand
the whole way up across the meadow
to the creek, where you should sit

a while to rest beneath a shade tree.
What boy could rest
in such unbridled light? Still, you sat
beside him, listening as the doors of this day
opened on another, on the village boy
your father was, who dawdled home

at twilight watching flocks of songbirds fall
into the sky reflected on a marsh pond,

reading for himself the day's last word
the moment it took flight. His was
a different world, of course, not this one
full of dangers watching like the eyes

of beasts between the trees. And you,
his son, were such a child your eyes
transformed the color of the sky
your parents lived beneath. To sit
beside the creek was close as you could come
to running wild, to catching frogs in ditches,

chasing meadowlarks. *You must not run,*
mein kind, what if you fall? The ditchwater
is dirty; if your shoes get wet you'll catch
the chills. And Mama's waiting,
she'll have sweets for you. Next morning
after rain, you watched a cloud of dragonflies dip

to a standing puddle, stitching up and down,
their touch not fluttering the surface.
You were too small for long pants
yet you sensed your only chance
to catch one was to hold your breath,
be absolutely still.

A Picture of my Father

The year I choose, as if the choice is mine, to keep you
in is 1939, a breath before the war, the year
you wore this face. It reaches me like an envelope

addressed in long-forgotten writing: three-piece tweed suit,
firmly knotted tie, your hair that won't lie flat, each feature
both familiar and oracular. Fifteen years old, and not the worst

of times. The grades you make come easy, and the subway
drops you near your father's candy store to make a meal of nuts
and hopjes, mix a phosphate, and pretend to work. A good son

to the man beyond the picture's edge, younger than I am now,
wiping his spectacles on the hem of his white apron. Business
is lousy, but then every business has been. Anyway, streetlights

are coming on. Soon you'll walk home together, down
the Grand Concourse, stopping for challah on a Friday night,
not talking much. You'll pass the park and turn on Morris,

entering the building where even the elevator smells of cabbage.
Home: The two rooms and a tiny kitchen that your parents
earned with thirty years of labor. A good son, you eavesdrop

on the homely talk, the headlines from the *Daily Forward,*
as you study at the table that your father bought your mother
when they wed. What am I missing in this story? Soon,

you'll graduate, enlist. The world go up in flames. The world
that birthed your parents bleed to death, the way your father finally
will bleed his life into the bathtub. If the choice was mine,

I'd keep you here forever, never empty-handed,
never begging history to wait.

Basic Training

Pens and tablets laid like cutlery before them,
Sol and Chaie sat across the kitchen table
spelling English words to tell their son
his leaving pulled a cord, night parachuted open,
they were falling fast. Little point in writing

anything. Even the sky was sorry
to look down on distances like these.
But what else did they have save old world flourishes
and swoops below the line to trace
his steps away? His footfalls

down the platform, arm in arm with fate,
three steps up to the train at Pennsylvania Station
where he paused to draw the magic circle
of their love so tight around him breath caught
in his chest like smoke. A dozen sleepless hours

the locomotive pressed the darkness back.
The next day passed. He spoke to no one,
staring out as mountains slouched to red clay hills ,
at last a beaten plain where he stepped down,
his jaw set hard. So every day at mail call

came a note from home: *regards from Ed,*
Aunt Sadie, Moe Levine; Gut Yontif on Sukkot,
a hot mean day like any other day
at Fort Benning, 1943; at last
his parents' plan to close up shop one Saturday,

hop on a train to Georgia, make it back to New York
Monday morning, *keine tsores,* forty-eight whole hours
departure to return. My father's heart knew well
the flourishes and swoops of words he carefully avoided
writing home, of brittle figures folded

into every line: night fell, and still he sat
by flashlight, spelling new descriptions for the bars
and brothels, *one swell town, you'd love it;*
men he later called "a bunch of psychopaths,"
fun-loving guys; his homesickness and fear, *I'm busy,*

Mom and Pop. Stay home and write to me.

War Stories

I.

Night was worst. If you lit a smoke,
its tiny star steered German shells
straight to you. They were close

as shadows, every voice so clear
you could take down their names.
The clink and gurgle of their big canteens

drove you wild with thirst. Even
their foxholes, deep, with logs across the top
beat ones where GIs huddled hugging rifles,

wet socks hung around necks to dry, feet rotting,
lice and dysentery, pinned down constantly
by fire, vertiginous exhaustion...

I've heard a hundred stories.
None comes from my father.

II.

Every night at six I waited for him.
Hopping on the stoop, I made believe
that I had wings to spread, that I could fly
up through the layerings of light,
the sunset pinks and golds, the world

would fall away like history. At last
his grey Dodge nudged the curb; his door
swung open, slammed. I made believe
my shadow, dancing out ahead of me
as I raced to his arms, was someone's ghost,

that it passed right through his body
when he caught me in a sweaty hug.
What a damn long day, he growled, the same thing
every day, then swung me to the clouds,
my skinny legs kicking with all their might

to rise. "Again! Again!" I pestered.
No, Hon — Daddy's tired. A moment later
he'd be slouching on the sofa, swallowing
his first long pull of Carling's Black Label
as the Huntley-Brinkley Report came on.

I settled at his feet. Hum-humming
to my dolls, binding their bodies
beautifully in homemade rainbow scraps,
I made believe a magic prince would come
for each of them, his winged horse

soaring through a secret cleft of light
between the clouds. My father downed
another beer and got a third. His tie hung loose
and limp. Flying above this world
my dolls smiled down on him

and on the newsmen gesturing at maps
of tiny missiles pin-pricked like gold stars
across a red island, at constellations massed
and twinkling in a distant land which glowed

red even on the black and white TV.

My dolls swooped with their loves
through towering purple clouds, so high
and far they could not hear my father:
Just drop the bomb and get it over with.
This whole damned country's gone to hell already

in a hand-basket. I made believe
they never would come down. Then
at six-thirty sharp, my mother called us in
to supper and I flew, so hungry
for the peace of meat and bread.

III.

Here's a story I have known since I was small:
once, when my father fought in Europe
some damn fool lieutenant ordered him
to burn a brush pile red with poison ivy.
An order is an order: every gold flame stung,
unwinding oil to smoke. My father held
his breath, a dampened handkerchief
across his face. But shells rained down

around him: his lungs filled with a gasp, a sob,
screams blooming in the din. For all he knew,
these were his last night's stars. When he woke
beneath a crucifix on a white wall
each breath fanned flames inside him. Burnt out
like a stump, he lay six weeks in hospital...
six weeks in which his unit burned
and bled to death in the Ardennes

IV.

and he alone survived to tell it.
Where'd you get that story?
What a load of crap.

You told it to me. Maybe it was Mom.
You've always had a great
imagination, Kid.

You mean I can't believe it?
My parents taught me not to waste
a goddamn thing. Someone is hungry
somewhere. Wing-nuts, safety pins,
a fold of foil, a snip of thread you may need
someday. You could do worse than to hold on
to scraps and shine.

What was the army like?
A bunch of Jew-haters and thugs.

Did you kill anyone? *What if I did?*
Correct me if I'm wrong
but that's the point of war.

Did you see survivors?
Look at me. Beyond the camps
the war left worlds of wounded souls
roosting like crows, alone
in history. The taste of carrion,
I bet you can get used to it.

Will you tell me your story?
I could tell you war stories, believe me.
I had some lucky breaks, just scraps
of luck so thin you can read through them
like wet newsprint. Lousy jokes
nobody laughs at. What a load of crap.
The punch line is the future, Kid. That's you.

V.

In the war, my father was a gunner.
I am sure that's true. He fought in Europe
and in the Pacific, came back home

to finish college, marry, raise a family
(that's me). Believe me, I could tell you
war stories. But that's a scrap, a joke. In truth

I was afraid to ask him anything. I'd lie awake
among my dolls pretending I could call for him,
never really calling, hoping he would hear

a fearful whisper, my breath shining
in the dark. And some nights he would.
He'd come and sit with me. He'd sing

a tuneless song in Yiddish, stroke my hair
and tell me I was lucky to be me: I was alive,
he said, and I was healthy, not to mention

smart and beautiful. And when he was a child
he didn't have what I had, not his own bedroom,
not even his own bed, I should be happy.

He told me he could never sleep at night
curled in his blankets on the living room divan,
eavesdropping on his parents, aunts and uncles

when they drank. Their voices pulled him down
like drowsiness into the past, into the shadows
of illicit loves, false documents, midnight

escapes, into the company of forgers, stowaways,
deceivers, men with no idea what waited
at the bottom of each cliff they leapt from.

It made me sad, he said. *My parents were*
good people. Quiet people. Life goes on.
Why talk about the past?

The Only Jewish Family in the Neighborhood

Out back, my mother pins old shirts
to lines, their white arms waving
off the sparrows. My sister laughs
with her. This year the puddle
spring pours in the gully is so deep
ducks come, a hatch of tadpoles
wriggles. I make boats of walnut shells
and chewing gum, a toothpick
mast, and set my paper sails to catch
light wings of wind, to sail across
the surface of my life the way these words
set out to cross the page, a tremolo
of thought. My sister calls my name
and leaps off of the swing, her body pausing
in mid-flight before Earth hugs her
to its breast again. She is afraid
of nothing. I am still,
like any sailor, studying the sky:
puffs of cumulus, the bashful sun.
The kids next door always insist
that Heaven is a cloud, so beautiful
the dead give thanks for dying, but no
Father's hand extends to me, no angel
chorus sings, unless you count
the rain I hear sometimes against my window,
complicating sleep as its words
strike night's surface. The kids
next door chase us and tell us
that we're damned; they pinch

with fingernails, pull hair. My father's
shirts fill with the nothingness
of angels, and my small boats
tip. I close my lids to keep
a world of silent faces in.

Oi Vei

Once when I tripped on the stairs
my grandmother came running:
Oi vei! Oi vei! she cried
the way the cantor sings it
on Yom Kippur, when all the sins
of mankind lie before him,
not a clumsy teenage granddaughter
embarrassed by the fuss. *Oi vei,*
indeed: my grandmother
would walk through fire for me,
and then make sure the whole world
heard about it. I was thirteen
and positive that no one
in all of human history felt
what I felt, no one had ever
loved or lied or pouted
in the mirror longing for a life
so full no simple body
can contain it. Even had I
broken both my legs in falling
I would have danced up
from the floor to prove
to her that I was not like her,
that her love fit my young life
like a tourniquet. Although
I loved her, and I knew
I loved her, I made sure to say
that I was *fine, thank you,*
and loud enough for all
the world to hear.

Going Back

Late in life, my Grandma's thoughts strayed back
more often to her village, Meskaporichi, never mind
it likely sunk back into marshland sixty years before.
Her siblings all were dead. She'd long since lost
track of her age and birthday, having traded both

to marry while her older sisters tripped the lights
with shady new world men. Still, once a year
my father held a birthday dinner for her
in a restaurant with candles, linen tablecloths and napkins,
with starchy waiters bowing in black frock coats. My parents

sparkled, kibitzing about *unindicted co-conspirators*
and secretarial contortions that erased dirt
from the surface of the past like an old rag, while I
sat fussing with more silverware than any person needs
and Grandma drifted from us: the dimmed lights

and hushed tones ushered in sweet echoes of her favorite hour,
the hour her father closed his shop, its aromatic chests
of linens sleeping as the sun slipped down,
another Shabbat woke. Soon she was no more with us
in that restaurant than we were at her parents' table

where her father's features glowed with pride
as if the moon itself reflected his beaming face:
such daily miracles his life was blessed with!
Eleven healthy children, shoes and coats, bread
on the table every night, a fine stout wife, a little flock

of goats who danced and kicked their heels up
on the steep sod roof and gave them milk. This was before,
of course, the boycotts and the burnings, in the days
of bounded plenty when a Jew could plow a field
he didn't own, or peddle wares, or simply be

a poor man in the Pale in safety. Now I wish too late
I'd listened close enough to feel that I was standing there
among her siblings as they sang the blessings, watched
the play of candlelight, smelled challah oven-warm. I wish
I'd sensed that every step we take we tread on bones.

But I was young and certain time's slow horses plodded
on without me, going back to someplace old like Meskaporichi
where my Grandma's thoughts dwelled, where a tiny hoof
broke through, a leg kicked at the beams above the Shabbat table,
and up in the dark a trapped kid floundered, crying for its life.

Kaddish

May His great Name grow exalted
and sanctified
                    though my grandfather
(may he rest in peace) on the eve of leaving
home, a dark wing shadowing the fields,
believed that God stayed put, and never spared
a glance over his shoulder, beckoning

in the world He created as He willed,
                                        the world
he ached and hungered for, in which a man could praise
a new moon rising over new land in a language
lit with questions no one in the shtetl dared to dream.

May He give reign to his kingship
in your lifetimes and your days
as every morning riding on the subway,
underworlds of print and free-thought yielded
shining veins of reason to his eyes

and in the lifetimes of the entire family
of Israel
            and every dusk before the air-shaft window
he'd hold forth to teach his young bride
what the Holy Books would not
swiftly and soon.
                    They bore a son
and trained their eyes like searchlights on his future.
Blessed, praised, glorified, exalted, extolled,

mighty, upraised, and lauded be the Name
of the Holy One, Blessed be He.
Although the boy
learned little Hebrew and was no Bar Mitzvah,
in his thirteenth year they threw a party, dancing,
their fine son bobbing upon a chair above their heads

beyond any blessing and song

that echoed in their thoughts on Shabbat when, perhaps,
they looked up for the moon before the sun had set to see
what can't be seen, although they longed for it to be there.

May there be abundant peace from Heaven
mingled with the things no telling of the story
changes: the War; the son's departure; the girlfriend
with her rosary; the diagnosis, the decline, the hollowness
that takes a husband's shape
and life
upon us and upon all Israel
even on the day
three decades later when the son stood helpless
in a borrowed yarmulke beside his mother's grave,
the Kaddish ready in transliteration on his tongue. And God
stayed put again inside the Rabbi's pocket as he told us,

"Save the Kaddish. You've no minyan here
to mourn for her."
Amen.

III.

"We die as many times as we close our eyes on memory."

—Fela Warshaw

Correspondence

"A well-known local doctor....escaped from
the ghetto, but was brought back and tortured.
'Who was with you?' she was asked by the SS on
16 June 1943. 'All of my people were with me,'
she replied, and then she was shot."
— a survivor of the Minsk Ghetto

I.

He saved a scattering
of old world postcards
posed in studios. In one:
three handsome soldiers rest
"at ease" in uniforms
before a painted curtain's
phony pastorale. There's no
decrypting now the smudge
of signature below a greeting
in Cyrillic script: *With regards,*
dear Brother Solomon
15 May 1928
Eastern Mountains.

And here's a dapper man,
in a modern tie and jacket,
thick black hair swept up,
who writes *I send respects*
to cousin Solomon and his darling family
from Hirschel Katzman
Kharkov, 22 January 1932.

My favorite's this young woman
with bobbed hair and spectacles

before a background so dark
it's as if no world surrounds her.
Every character's deliberate,
the way a child would write:
Warm wishes to dear Solomon
from your loving niece,
your Pessy Rivka
15 October 1935
(You would agree that I am prettier
than this photograph!)

Not all are legible. A slick-haired
mustached man in high-shined shoes
sits on a rough birch gate. The back's
a scrawl of faded Yiddish.
1938. His name
is Bursztyn. That is all
I'll ever know of him.

II.

Dear brother-cousin-uncle-
friend-grandfather Solomon,
could you have told me
how the stories of these people
end? There must have been
so many letters calling you
to look back and face the world
you left behind, although
you'd blown away
like pollen on the wind
across new fields. And maybe
with the years the letters

spoke to you when you woke
in the night to count
again, again, what you had lost
and found. Did Avram write details
of the beatings, boycotts,
how he longed to follow you,
he'd pay you back with interest?
Did pretty Pessy Rivka's mother
beg you, for god's sake,
at least send passage for the children
as their future dropped
like sand inside an hourglass
into the past? Or did the letters
never warn you of the worst
to come, anymore than anyone
in Meskaporichi had a warning,
waking up one lush June day
in 1942 to orders
herding Jews into the city,
into the ghetto, into a meter and half
of space per person (none allowed
for children), into terror,
into utter silence?

And even had you known,
what could you do?
Through one long winter
of the Great Depression
you wore two tattered coats
and peddled roasted chestnuts
in Times Square. Your second
shop had failed. You borrowed
for the third. You knew from hunger.
So what ticket could you buy?

And what name
would you write on it?
Your mother, gazing wanly
from old photographs
with eyes about to close?
A niece or cousin? What about
your sister, crippled
in the 1921 pogrom?

III.

The future drops into the past:
that's history. A single
lush June day in 1942
was long enough
to transport all the Jews
from Meskaporichi.
Within two years
(he could not know this until later)
there was no one left.
Solomon's third shop, though,
did well enough despite
the rationing. I picture him,
a small, soft-featured man
in shirtsleeves in a darkened room.
He sits, wiping his eyes.
The bedstead creaks
as ghosts lie down to rest
beside him.

IV.

When I was a child, I loved
the Pesach service best.
I loved to say out loud, "This is because
of what the Lord did for *me*
when *I* was delivered
from slavery in the land
of Egypt." I understood
that I was there:
this was my story.
Now I say out loud
this poem is for my grandfather
because of what he did for *me*
when *I* was delivered
from the shtetls, ghettoes,
camps, delivered from the cellars
and the forests. On the ticket
he could not afford to buy,
the one he never sent
in answer to the letters
long since lost, the name he wrote
is mine.

To Be a Jew

In every scene I script for Sol and Chaie,
Shabbat candles burn. I say the prayer in Hebrew
as I light them, as the wayward flames
arrange the room of memory around them.

This is a debt I owe, a ritual of love. My grandfather
was meant to be a rabbi, as his grandfather was:
not just a learned man but one whose prayers
would resonate within time's hollow body

like a lute. Beyond the synagogue
a man like him had neither land nor rights:
to be a Jew was to be ever lonely,
even in the shtetl where God wandered

like a summer breeze. In every memory I have
or think I have, my grandparents shine
with Jewishness: with Yiddish words
spicing their English, with their books,

their kitchen smells. To be the Jew I am
is to be ever outside looking in at others
who themselves are ever outsiders. If God
was in the shul in Meskaporichi, perhaps he stayed behind

as Solomon stowed away, washed up
in New York City, traded Talmud for a high school
education; if God was flexible, perhaps he shlepped
his bundles up the gangplank, stayed awake and sang

a lullaby to Chaie's baby brothers.
Either way, my grandparents landed alone
in a century when what was left of God
went up the smokestacks over Sobibor,

when, to be a Jew, I burn the Shabbat candles
that they never lit in New York City,
never mind my fabrications. And in the flames
I light my wish to dwell among them.

Meskaporichi

In my parents' cupboard sat a tarnished
silver goblet inscribed *Meskaporicher*
Mutual Aid Society. It came out each Pesach
of my childhood to stand

upon the seder plate, surrounded
by a world of metaphor: the paschal lamb;
the roasted egg and karpas for spring's
promises; matzo for haste and hunger;

marror and charoset, bitter with the sweet.
The goblet held Elijah's share
of wine. He never came for it.
Next morning, I would pick it up

and wonder whose hands wore
the plating through, whose lips had touched
the rim. I wanted to believe my grandfather
was there, a genie in a lamp. He was

a mystery, a feature of the past
that no one spoke of but in tones
that hushed like rain. He was an exile
from the sweet myth of a homeland

that was never mine. I was almost grown
before the cup's inscription struck me
with its meaning: *No one fled*
alone. The vanished world itself

had rooted in the new with my grandparents
like a spring bulb: friends and neighbors,
relatives, the rabbi in his crow-black coat,
voices that once called down the muddy streets

of Meskaporichi came to hawk produce
and meat and shoes from New York shops
and pushcarts. What I'd known before
of my grandparents' history

was loneliness; when I asked
my father what he knew of Meskaporichi
he said, *There's nothing left.* I was
no older when I asked

than my grandparents were
a century ago back in the shtetl
before this cup was made,
before it overflowed

with people's lives.

My Dearest Parents,

May these words find you
still among the living. Would you know me
now? I close my eyes to meet yours,
Father: in your stiff black Shabbat suit

and silken cap, your gaze is deep
as I remember it, a tzaddik's gaze
above your beard gone white. How
did you let me go? And Mother,

by his side as ever you have been,
your kind square face framed
by a kerchief: every day
my son fought overseas, I pictured you

as if my heart held photographs
and prayed aloud. The worst
is over now, they say, but I know
better. I can hear the wings

of vultures fanning ash and ember,
keening voices rising into clouds
of smoke. At least my son
is coming home. My son. He writes

to me: Hell's bells, Poppa,
I never want you even to imagine
what has happened here. *As if*
I did not know how shadows flex

and spread within the human soul.
As if my heart has room for anything
but dybbuks roaming its dim lanes
and weeping. Father, Mother,

I must let you go. These words
will never find you.

1945

A summer evening on the roof
 on Morris Avenue: the sky a pale
skin over the city's sculpted hollows
 falling dark. Flanked by his parents,

my young father stares into the camera,
 his head inflected forward. He is home
on leave after VE Day: the troopship convoy
 chuffed into New York Harbor

washed with spotlights, music,
 toilet paper streamers, pretty girls
(one of whom would later be
 my mother) glad to kiss any GI

they got their hands on... But this evening
 all he's thinking of is shipping out
tomorrow for the Philippines.
 Given the choice, who wouldn't settle

for time stopping with the shutter's
 click? His father angles toward him,
slightly built and frail; no expression
 sails his lips' horizon. Has he told his son

that life is shipping out, his time is short?
 Did they sit like strangers, silent
on the subway to Bronx Hospital
 where doctors named their fears?

To my father's right, his mother. Her eyes hold
        a darkness so particular it's hard
to look: they are curators
        of care. In this, the last picture

I have of the three of them together
        dusk is falling and my father hugs
his parents before another parting,
        and another parting.

Last Words

When you were ten years old
I caught you peeking out
from underneath the tablecloth
at me. Your brothers sang
half-heartedly, nodding like turtles
in the ditches. What the Torah asks
of us is that we mouth each word
as if our lives hang on it,
never mind who's watching,
as you practiced in the night
your thin voice rising
like a slip of moon.
My Chaiele, life hangs
on things we can not learn.
Torah is not enough to keep me
from what I have lost. Forgive me:
you are handsome; our grown son
will care for you. The dead
already shift to make a space
for me within the ruins
of the world to come.

Understanding the Prognosis

"Patients with idiopathic Parkinson's typically develop bradykinesia, festination, and tremors, plus secondary symptoms including dysphagia, incontinence, hypophonia, microphagia, seborrhea, hyperhidrosis, and bradyphrenia. Psychosocial symptoms may include anxiety, depression, and a sense of isolation."

Hands shake like moths. Feet shuffle
in a parody of dance. Each impulse
to the brain is slow as drying clay.

The face becomes a rigid mask. The head
hangs forward and the shoulders droop
(the easy trope is "posture of defeat").

Falling is common. Speech draws close
to silence; questions vanish into time
before an answer forms. Because control

of muscles lapses like a lease, drooling
and soiling of one's self are to be
expected. Even breath caught in the throat

can suffocate. The mind remains intact.
It reads the news, feels fearful for the son
at war, the wife worn out with care,

the loss of income, in the certainty
that nothing will get better. A dark space
opens slowly in the heart.

Psalm 23:4

I walk through the valley
My grandmother chose
two cabbages, stopped in at Sadie's
for a glass of tea, and on the way home
to his sick-room bought a fish
that smelled fresh, never knowing this day
would be different from all other days.

of the shadow
My grandfather's hands quaked
like a taut string bowed, like rolling dice,
like butter in a churn, like fear itself,
as he rose from the chair she left him in
and stumbled to the bathroom. A thrifty man,
he stripped down, folded shirt and trousers
not to ruin them.

of death
That morning sang to him
in a way that every sorrow of his life
danced to, as his fingers danced
along the bone handle, the carbon steel blade
she had given him the day they wed
and warm bath water hugged him.

I will fear no evil
She laid her coat across a kitchen chair,
set down her parcels, turned the kettle on,
knocked at the door and called his name

before turning the knob. Like smoke
that moment tinges every breath I take

for thou art with me
always.

Last Words

Forgive me. In the mirror I see
nothing. Already I'm a ghost.
If any part of me remained
as you once knew me
I would carry on
this heavy sack, my body.
But life taught me early
how to say goodbye. Perhaps
I am the mirror
with nobody looking in.
Perhaps I am a road, my own
way home; you are
the only landmark I still know.
All that is left for me
because I love you, is the time
it takes to draw the bath.
To be wept clean of life.

Introducing Myself in Middle Age to My Grandfather

There was a time I walked in your cold city
          and saw death
                    around me everywhere. Sometimes it rose

behind my eyes
          to meet the gaze of beggars in the subway; other times
                    it came from nowhere

like the girl who leapt out of a twelfth floor window
          to my feet. She was
                    as beautiful as I was then, as full, no doubt

of bitter questions.
          But I left that place intact. I wed a man
                    like winter melting

into spring, whose loneliness embraced
          my own. We saw
                    the world, came home to one another

drew lots with the future,
          praying for the long end. Let me tell you,
                    it's not easy

shedding skins like those I've worn; the body
          longs to dance
                    on its own grave, the Earth keeps turning

us through empty space.

When I was small, I carried in my heart
a dead grandfather,

with his latticework of myths and what I came to see
as lies. But how
I loved to close my eyes and see you circling

the world I knew,
exiled from me, perhaps, but perfect
as my life

was meant to be. It never was, of course; I always
smelled the smoke
from burning villages, from steamship stacks,

from crematoria
and I was scared. And somehow I grew up
not understanding

that you took your life, that all the grief
my father swallowed with his pills each night
could not dissolve the darkness. Now I've borne

your name and face
into the world my children walk, a world
you wouldn't recognize, as dangerous

and sweet as any. And I've a debt to pay:
to give you back
your death; to give you back your life.

GLOSSARY AND NOTES

Baruch atah adonai — Invocation that begins many Hebrew prayers.

cheder — An elementary Torah school.

dybbuk — The restless soul of a dead person that enters the body of a living person and takes possession.

Etel Betel's tochter und Chaim Yankel's zohn — The first line of a comic Yiddish song.

golem — An artificial person given life by the carving of a Sacred Name upon his or her forehead. Has deeper meanings in some Hebrew Mysticism, in which we are all golems in some sense.

Gut yontif — Holiday greeting.

Kaddish — A Jewish prayer, recited by mourners.

keine tsores — No trouble.

meine sheyne maidlakh — My pretty little girls.

minyan — Ten Jewish men, the quorum necessary to recite certain prayers.

mitzvot — Teachings based on the Torah. In Yiddish, "mitzvah" means good deed.

pogrom — Organized attack on Jews, frequent in

19th and early 20th century Eastern Europe.

pogromschik — Participant in a pogrom.

shiksa — Non-Jewish woman.

sh'ma — The most well-known prayer of Jewish liturgy.

shiva — Immediately upon the burial of a loved one, family members observe an initial mourning period of seven (*shiva*, in Hebrew) days.

shtetl — *S*mall Jewish towns of Eastern Europe.

shul — Yiddish for synagogue.

Talmud — The authoritative body of Jewish law and tradition, supplementing scriptural law.

Torah — The first five books of the Hebrew bible portions of which are read every Sabbath.

tzaddik — A righteous person.

* * *

"Shoes in Meskaporichi" (p.20) grew out of images from Roman Vishniac's book, *A Vanished World.*

"Affadavit of the Master or Commanding Officer"(p. 23) is based upon period documents required of steamship captains.

"War Stories" (p. 64) is inspired by passages from *Citizen Soldiers* by Stephen Ambrose.

CPSIA information can be obtained at www.ICGtesting.com
Printed in the USA
BVOW03s1317120315

391448BV00001B/7/P

9 781934 999523